STORYBOOKS TEACH
ABOUT WORLD CULTURES

by Tanya Lieberman

Illustrated by Adam Weisblatt

This book is dedicated to:
Abby, Anna, & Mila

Publisher: Roberta Suid
Copy Editor: Carol Whiteley
Production: Santa Monica Press

For a complete catalog of our products,
please write to the address below:
P.O. Box 1680, Palo Alto, California 94302

Monday Morning is a registered trademark of
Monday Morning Books, Inc.

ISBN 1-878279-77-7

Printed in the United States of America

987654321

❖ CONTENTS ❖

❖ INTRODUCTION ❖

Language, dress, food, music, beliefs, customs—all are part of what we know as culture. And while you may have to travel thousands of miles to take part in a game of pok-a-tok or dance the saravan, information about the culture and folklore of many lands is as near as your closest library or bookstore.

Storybooks Teach About World Cultures is a resource that brings such information to your classroom. In each chapter you'll find:
- *Story Summaries* that allow you to sample folklore storybooks in advance.
- *Discovery/Exploration* ideas and activities related to the featured storybooks and cultures.
- *Language Links* that present language-based activities based on the chosen storybooks and cultures.

Learning Objectives

Exposure to different cultures can be a fascinating process of discovery for children—it may encourage a lifelong interest and appreciation in people's differences and similarities. Through exploration of different societies students can gain:
- **knowledge** of the history, geography, and culture of different civilizations;
- **respect** for the diversity as well as the commonality of all peoples, and the ability to separate stereotype from reality;
- **skills** for living in a global society, such as communication, tolerance, problem solving, and cooperation; and
- **concern** for the future of all people.

Teaching Strategies

Culture is a complex institution to teach as well as to learn. To help make your teaching more successful:
- Allow students to **process** each new experience. Experiencing something new or different can make anyone uncomfortable. Talk over experiences so that ideas that first seem strange or funny can be understood in their proper context.
- Give students a **framework** for understanding differences by introducing concepts such as values, beliefs, and social organization.
- Draw **connections** between the cultures you study and the past, our own lives in the present, and our global future.
- Use the **resources** of your classroom and the local community to enable students to see, hear, smell, taste, and touch many cultures. A trip to a local import shop or a presentation by someone who has just been abroad can make culture come alive for your students.

Books on Teaching About World Cultures

Meagher, Laura. *Teaching Children About Global Awareness.* New York: Crossroad, 1991.

Tiedt, Pamela L., and Tiedt, Iris M. *Multicultural Teaching.* Boston: Allyn and Bacon, 1990.

❖ PART I ❖

Africa

If culture is a form of wealth, Africa is a rich land. From the "talking drum" festivals of the Ewe to the storytelling tradition of the Malinese "griots," the diversity of African culture stretches the imagination. African culture is as brilliant as Kente cloth, and as precious as the dolls Sotho women carry on their marriage day.

But what is it like to live in Africa? You can give students a taste of the cultural strengths as well as some of the daily challenges of African life through exploration and study. Can your students balance objects on their heads, the way that African children do? Have them give it a try. What is it like to live in an African home? Encourage your students to discover more about African life by reading the selected storybooks in this chapter:

• The African version of the Cinderella fairy tale can help teach about this culture by contrasting it with the familiar version.

• Folklore about Anansi the Spider and the Trickster Rabbit of West Africa will give insight into the entertaining side of African literature.

• Songololo, Ntombi, and Zamani, the stars of the picture books featured in this unit, will teach readers about the culture of the modern African market and the rites of passage of African children.

AFRICAN CINDERELLAS

Sometimes similarities make differences more visible. By contrasting African Cinderella stories with the Grimm version of the tale, children will become more aware of the distinctions of African culture.

As they listen to this familiar tale unfold, students will be struck by differences in names, dress, family, village life, and other elements of culture. But by using the familiar to expose students to new ideas, students may gain greater respect for those differences, and better understanding of the universality of the story's moral—no one likes to be sent to bed without supper!

To get the most out of this unit, you may first want to review the Grimm version of Cinderella with your students. This way, the story will be fresh in their minds. Then jump right into the African Cinderella stories.

The storybooks used in this unit are:

Climo, Shirley. *The Egyptian Cinderella*. New York: HarperCollins, 1989.
Phumla. *Nomi and the Magic Fish*. New York: Lothrop, 1987.

❖ ACTIVITIES ❖

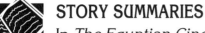 **STORY SUMMARIES**

In *The Egyptian Cinderella*, a Greek maiden named Rhodopis is sold into slavery in Egypt. The servant girls in the household treat her poorly, but her master gives her a pair of gold slippers to honor her grace. One day a falcon steals one of the slippers and brings it to the Pharaoh Anasis. The pharaoh accepts the shoe as a sign, and announces that he will marry the woman who can wear it. He searches the land for the owner, and when it fits only Rhodopis she becomes his bride.

Nomi and the Magic Fish is a Zulu Cinderella tale. In the story, Nomi's mother dies at Nomi's birth and her father remarries. Nomi's stepmother treats her cruelly. But one day a magic fish appears to Nomi and gives her food. When the stepmother learns of the fish, she captures and cooks it for dinner. Nomi saves the bones and places them in the Chief's garden. But when the Chief tries to pick them up, he can't. He announces that he will marry the girl who can pick up the bones, and when only Nomi can do so she becomes his wife.

 DISCOVERY/EXPLORATION

A storyteller in West Africa was once seen wearing a "storytelling hat." It was a wide-brimmed guinea corn straw hat, from which hung wood carvings, ivory, bits of fur, and even a leopard's tooth. Each object represented a story from the storyteller's repertoire. Anyone who wanted to hear a story simply picked an object, agreed on a price, and sat down to listen to the tale.

Your students can make their own storytelling hat. Have them pick a storybook (preferably an African story) that they would like to retell. Then have each of them fashion an object that represents something about the story (a drawing of a character, for example). Attach each child's object to the brim of a straw hat so that they dangle down. Then have students pick an object from the hat and have the creator recite his or her story to the rest of the class.

 LANGUAGE LINKS

Discuss the elements of a story (characters, plot, events, setting, etc.) with your class, and compare those elements in the Grimms' Cinderella to those in the African Cinderellas. How are the stories similar and different culturally? Discuss such things as family, village life, objects, dress, and the roles of men and women.

GOING TO MARKET

What is life like in Africa today? The storybooks in this chapter will help students find out, especially about life for their young counterparts: their families, songs, and dreams.

Students will also discover what it's like to go shopping in Africa, and how differently goods are bought and sold. In addition they'll learn about the differences between city and country life, and the kinds of challenges and rewards both types of life involve. The vivid illustrations in these storybooks also highlight elements of African culture.

Through the activities in this chapter, students can practice math skills while learning about a different way to shop, and compare their own rites of passage with those of children in Africa today.

The storybooks used in this unit are:

Daly, Niki. *Not So Fast, Songololo*. New York: Atheneum, 1986.
Feelings, Muriel L. *Zamani Goes to Market*. New York: Seabury, 1970.
Seed, Jenny. *Ntombi's Song*. Boston: Beacon, 1987.

❖ ACTIVITIES ❖

STORY SUMMARIES

In *Not So Fast, Songololo,* Malusi is a South African boy who likes to do things slowly. When his grandmother asks him to help her do her shopping, his worn-out "tackies" (tennis shoes) slow him down. In the city, Malusi is overwhelmed by the many cars, people, and stores. Grandma buys Malusi new shoes and he walks quickly home.

In *Zamani Goes to Market,* Zamani, a young Kenyan boy, is thrilled to go to the market with his father and the other adults. There he eyes a kanzu (traditional Kenyan shirt), but he decides to buy a present for his mother. His mother loves the present, and he discovers that his father has bought him the kanzu!

In *Ntombi's Song,* a South African girl named Ntombi wants to be grown up like her cousin. At her mother's request, Ntombi goes to the store to buy sugar, but on her way home she drops it! Ntombi must earn money to replace the sugar. In the market, she begins to sing and dance, and catches the attention of tourists who give her money to replace the sugar.

DISCOVERY/EXPLORATION

In many markets in Africa, prices are not fixed but negotiated between buyer and seller. Set up a marketplace in the classroom, and have half the students be vendors and the other half shoppers. Give the vendors objects to sell (such as marbles) and tell them that their goal is to sell as many items as they can for as much as they can. Give the shoppers some play money and tell them that their object is to buy as much as they can for as little as they can. Set them loose in the market to negotiate the best deal. Stop the activity when all the shoppers have made a purchase, and discuss the results.

LANGUAGE LINKS

In Africa there are many ways to honor the transition from childhood to adulthood. Among the Chagga people of East Africa, village priests in traditional costume perform a ceremony for groups of children whose faces have been painted. For the story characters Ntombi and Zamani, going to market is an adult task that represents maturity. Have students write a paragraph on what marks the passage into adulthood in their own culture: perhaps a driver's license, bar mitzvah, sweet sixteen party, being able to vote, or getting married. How do these things compare to African rites of passage?

TRICKSTER TALES

"Tricksters" are popular and delightful characters found in folk literature around the world, from Africa to the Pacific Islands to Europe to North and South America. Perhaps the two best-known African tricksters are Anansi the Spider (sometimes seen as a human being) and the Trickster Rabbit. In North America these schemers are known as Bre'r Rabbit and Aunt Nancy the Spider.

In Africa, the best-known trickster tales are from West African nations, though tricksters appear with different names in stories spanning the continent. These tales most often involve a scheme by Anansi or Trickster Rabbit to gain something they want, but most often the two are outwitted. Trickster stories usually involve teaching the audience a moral lesson.

In the following activities, students have the opportunity to be tricksters in their own right by playing an African children's game and by creating their own trickster tale.

The storybooks used in this unit are:

Kimmel, Eric A. *Anansi and the Moss-Covered Rock.*
New York: Holiday House, 1988.
McDermott, Gerald. *Zomo the Rabbit.* New York: Harcourt, 1992.

❖ ACTIVITIES ❖

STORY SUMMARIES

In *Anansi and the Moss-Covered Rock*, Anansi the Spider is walking in the forest when he comes upon a rock that makes him fall over senseless when he says, "Isn't this a strange rock..." Anansi goes straight to Lion's house, and brings him to the rock. When Lion is knocked out, Anansi steals his store of yams. Anansi plays this trick on Elephant, Hippopotamus, and every other animal in the forest. But when he tries his trick on Little Bush Deer, she tricks him into saying the magic words. When Anansi falls over, the other animals retrieve their food.

Zomo the Rabbit is searching for wisdom. He asks the Sky-God for it and is promised his reward if he can bring the god three things: the scales of the big fish, milk from the wild cow, and the tooth of the leopard. Zomo rushes to the ocean and plays a drum, which causes the fish to dance. While dancing, the fish loses all of his scales. Zomo then provokes the wild cow into charging after him, and while the cow is stuck in a tree he steals her milk. Finally, Zomo leaves his prizes on the road as a trap for the leopard, who slips on them and loses a tooth. When Zomo presents the treasures to the Sky-God, he is given wisdom—that three things worth having are courage, good sense, and caution.

DISCOVERY/EXPLORATION

Here's an opportunity for students to be tricksters in a simple but fun children's game from West Africa. To play "Dosu," have the first group of three or more sit in a sandbox. Give one student an object, such as a penny, bean, or marble. This player should bury the object in a pile of loose sand, then form more piles of sand until there are as many piles as players. Each player chooses a pile, and the one who finds the object is the next to hide it. Discuss with the class the kinds of games we create out of our own environment, such as hopscotch on pavement, and what we can infer about the lives of African children from playing "Dosu."

LANGUAGE LINKS

Discuss the elements of African trickster stories with your students. Anansi and Trickster Rabbit always attempt to outwit someone, but in the end they are usually outsmarted. Trickster stories are often designed to teach the listeners a moral, and are always entertaining. Have students identify these elements in the storybooks, then let them create their own trickster story.

PART 2

Asia

Asia is a land of great cultural and geographical diversity. From the plateaus of Inner Mongolia to the rain forests of Indonesia, Asia accounts for one-third of the land mass of the world and two-thirds of its population. It contains the world's highest peak, Mount Everest, and the world's lowest land surface, the shore of the Dead Sea. Asia is home to the neon-lit streets of Tokyo as well as villages still without electricity and running water.

This chapter provides a jumping-off point for the exploration of Asia through lessons on Asian concepts of time, heroic adventure, and family.

• The first unit deals with ancient elements of the 4,000-year-old Chinese culture—the lunar calendar and the zodiac—which are still respected in China and other Asian countries today.

• The second unit allows students to explore the cultural traditions of Japan through storybooks depicting heroic adventures and exercises, bringing to life the traditions of the country.

• The final unit gives students a peek at today's Asian families through storybooks depicting modern-day Vietnam, India, and Hong Kong. How important are families in Asian cultures? And how do they compare to your students' families?

THE CHINESE ZODIAC

The Chinese year has 354 days, with 12 months of 29 or 30 days each. The difference between this calendar and the solar calendar has been compensated for by the addition of weeks or even months at certain intervals. At the calendar's origin, the new year began when a new moon was closest to the constellation Aquarius, usually between January 20 and February 18. According to Chinese folklore, the lunar calendar was developed in 2698 B.C. to help farmers plant and harvest at the best times. The calendar was so important that the emperor himself was responsible for issuing it.

The calendar has a 12-year cycle, with an animal representing each year. The Chinese believe that people born in a particular year exhibit the characteristics of their animal sign. The storybooks in this unit involve one or more of the 12 legendary animals.

While the people in China today operate on the solar calendar, the lunar calendar and the zodiac symbols remain important in daily life. Decisions on marriage, friendship, and business are still made according to sign. And if someone asks how old you are, the answer "I'm a rooster" will be understood!

The storybooks used in this unit are:

Van Woerkom, Dorothy. *The Rat, the Ox, and the Zodiac.* New York: Crown, 1976.
Wallace, Ian. *Chin Chiang and the Dragon's Dance.* New York: Atheneum, 1984.

13

❖ ACTIVITIES ❖

STORY SUMMARIES

In *The Rat, the Ox, and the Zodiac*, Emperor Shun Yu faces a dilemma: will the rat or the ox be the first animal in the zodiac? The ox is strong, the emperor is told, but the rat is clever. The emperor delegates the decision to the other 10 animals of the zodiac. But their votes are equally divided, so the emperor puts the question to the people. Rat complains that no one will see him because of his small size, so he is made bigger. The people, on seeing such a big rat, choose him as the first animal in the zodiac.

In *Chin Chiang and the Dragon's Dance,* young Chin Chiang dreams of dancing the dragon's dance in the new year parade. This year is the Year of the Dragon, and though Chiang practices diligently with his grandfather he feels too clumsy. Chiang meets an old woman, Pu Yee, and thinks that she can take his place in the dance. But when Chiang and Pu Yee go to the parade, he finds that he in fact can do the dance.

DISCOVERY/EXPLORATION

What year is it according to the lunar calendar? The year 2698 B.C. was the first year of that calendar, so, to figure out what year it is now, add 2698 to the current year. 1994, for example, is 4692 on the lunar calendar. Have your class calculate the answer with you using a timeline to demonstrate the principle.

Have more advanced students figure out how old they are by the Chinese calendar. In China everyone turns one year older on the same day—New Year's Day, which usually falls in late January or early February. If you were born on October 18, 1985, you became 1 year old in January 1986.

LANGUAGE LINKS

What animal are you according to the zodiac? Have students look up their birth year on the illustration on page 13 and determine their animal and characteristics. Then discuss the qualities attributed to each animal. Have each student write a short essay on whether or not he or she fits the particular animal's description.

Rat: thrifty, quick-tempered.
Ox: stubborn, patient, trusting.
Tiger: sensitive, passionate.
Snake: deep thinker and soft-spoken.
Rabbit: affectionate and cautious.
Dragon: full of vitality and strength.

Horse: cheerful, perceptive, and quick-witted.
Sheep: strong beliefs, compassionate.
Monkey: inventor and improviser.
Rooster: sharp and neat.
Dog: loyal, trustworthy, and faithful.
Pig: studious, well-informed, reliable.

HEROIC TALES FROM JAPAN

The 17th century in Japan was the age of the samurai. Warlords ruled the country, and the samurai were the most respected and feared warriors in the land. While your students may have heard of ninjas and the "samurai sword," they may not know that the samurai also led a peacetime life that included meditation, garden design, and even poetry.

Many samurai were Buddhists, who believed in improving themselves through meditation. They could also often be found gazing silently over a garden of their own design. Hundreds of years later, samurai-designed gardens still serve peaceful functions in Japanese society: as places of quiet contemplation and places to marvel at the beauty of nature.

The truly great samurai was admired for his skill with words as well as war. Poetry writing, particularly haiku, is a lesser-known pastime of these warriors. The haiku poem was developed in the 17th century, and has become one of the most admired poetic forms in the world.

The storybooks used in this unit are:

San Souci, Robert D. *The Samurai's Daughter*. New York: Dial, 1992.
Shute, Linda. *Momotaro*. New York: Lothrop, Lee and Shepard, 1986.

❖ ACTIVITIES ❖

 ## STORY SUMMARIES

In *The Samurai's Daughter,* Tokoyo is raised by her father to know both the skills of the samurai and the pastimes befitting a lady of the time. Tokoyo much prefers the life of the amas, the brave women divers who collect pearls and shellfish from the bottom of the ocean. When Tokoyo's father is banished to an island by an emperor who is possessed by an evil spirit, she braves the ocean to save him.

In *Momotaro,* a childless Japanese couple pray for a child and receive a baby floating down the river inside of a peach. They name him Momotaro, or "peach boy." When Momotaro turns 15 he decides to go to the mountain of the Oni (ogres), who have terrorized the peasants of the land for years. His mother packs kibi dango (rice dumplings) for his journey. Along the way Momotaro meets a dog, a monkey, and a pheasant, who join him in return for his kibi dango. When the four reach the island of the Oni, they fight valiantly and defeat them, and return to their village to live in peace.

DISCOVERY/EXPLORATION

Your students can make their own Japanese gardens. Karesansui, or "dry mountain and water," are gardens that use lines in the sand to represent water. Show students pictures of Japanese gardens and discuss their significance in Japanese culture. Then give each student a thick paper plate, shoe box cover, or other smooth-surfaced material. In a sandbox, use a rake or stick to demonstrate how lines can be drawn in the sand to look like water. Make smooth, wavy lines to represent waves. Then let the children collect small rocks, pieces of tanbark, twigs, and other natural objects. In the classroom, have the students cover their plates with a layer of sand and design a garden with their objects; they can draw in the sand using pencils, chopsticks, or other implements. Play soft music, Japanese if available, while they work, or read a Japanese story. Remind the students that the miniature gardens should look natural—not too neat—and convey a message of tranquility, be pleasant to look at, and inspire thought.

LANGUAGE LINKS

Link your students' karesansui to a lesson in haiku poetry writing. Every haiku has 17 syllables, in three lines of 5, 7, and 5 syllables each. Haiku poems express a fragment of a scene or feeling; their simplicity is their power. Have each student write a haiku about the garden he or she made, and try to capture its meaning in simple, open-ended form.

THE FAMILY IN ASIA

The modern Asian family lives much as it has for centuries: together, with as many as three or four generations under the same roof. Asian people's names are written differently than in the west—the family name comes first. And many countries still follow traditions of ancestor worship, continuing to pay their respects to their elders even after they pass away.

The importance of the family in Asia is easily seen through language. In India, for example, languages have words for such familial relationships as a person's uncle who is younger than the person's father; such words don't exist in English. And in Cambodia, as in many Asian countries, there is no word for "you." Instead, the speaker must decide what to call a person based on his or her familial relationship with that person.

Confusing? Just remember what most Koreans, and most others Asian people, believe: family is the most important thing in life, and devotion to one's parents is the most important duty.

The storybooks used in this unit are:

Bonnici, Peter. *The Festival*. Minneapolis: Carolrhoda Books, 1985.
Lee, Jeanne M. *Ba Nam*. New York: Henry Holt, 1987.
Levinson, Riki. *Our Home Is the Sea*. New York: Dutton, 1988.

❖ ACTIVITIES ❖

STORY SUMMARIES

In *The Festival*, a young Indian boy, Arjuna, awaits the village festival during which he will take his place among the men in the village. During the festival he gets his first lungi (the sarong-style lower garment men wear in India) and dances with the men, but is horrified when the new lungi falls down! Arjuna is comforted by his grandfather and hot chapatis (bread-like crackers).

In *Ba Nam*, Nan, a young Vietnamese girl, is excited to finally be old enough to participate in Thanh Minh Day. With her mother and brother she goes to the graves of her ancestors to offer incense and other gifts to the spirits of the dead. She is frightened when she first meets Ba Nam (Ba means grandmother), the keeper of the graves of their ancestors, but is grateful when Ba Nam helps her family during a storm.

In *Our Home Is the Sea,* a young boy rushes home from school through the busy streets of Hong Kong. He takes a tram, runs through the park, and passes the market before arriving at the harbor. There his family waits in their fishing-boat home, where they all eat dinner together.

DISCOVERY/EXPLORATION

Families in Asia vary greatly in size from country to country. In this activity, students can practice their math and learn more about averaging while learning about family life in Asia. Have students read the following statistics, which show the number of people per household:

Japan: 3.2   Korea: 4.5   Singapore: 4.7   Philippines: 5.9   Burma: 5.2

Begin by helping your class locate each of these countries on the map. Then ask each student how many people are in his or her family, and together calculate the average number of persons per household. How does the student rate compare to the Asian rates above? Discuss the concepts of nuclear and extended families. Discuss the numbers presented, and how to interpret averages. How, for example, can you have 4.5 people? As an option, graph these figures along with your class' average.

LANGUAGE LINKS

In Vietnam, families keep a Ho Kau, or family register, which records all family members' births and deaths. Have your students develop their own Ho Kau by making a list of as many family members as possible. Parents may be enlisted in this effort.

PART 3

Australia

To European explorers in the 17th century, Australia was "Terra Australis Incognita," or the "Unknown Southern Land." To aboriginal peoples, it was a sacred homeland. To European settlers, it was a new and challenging land. And to those who inhabit Australia today, Australia is still a continent of many meanings.

For perhaps 40,000 years, Australia has been the homeland of aboriginal people. At the time of the first white settlement, 300,000 to 350,000 native Australians representing as many as 500 tribes lived on the continent. Their culture was largely a no-madic one, and had a strong relationship with the land. The people still believe in a period, called the "Dreamtime," in which their ancestors, in both human and animal form, roamed the land. These ancestors' paths, known to the members of each clan, are often called "songlines": tracks sometimes marked by features such as mountains or rocks, and sometimes invisible. Aborigines still honor those lines, and to this day go on "walkabouts," retrac-ing those invisible paths across the land.

What will Australia mean to your students? The storybooks selected for this chapter will expose them to both the aboriginal and the settler cultures, and help them develop their own visions of this exciting land.

STORIES FROM THE DREAMTIME

Every culture has a "creation story." The Australian aborigines' version is an elaborate set of legends from a long-ago period called the Dreamtime.

According to the legends, the earth was created when the original ancestors descended from the stars. They were the only creatures on earth and had supernatural powers. They created the natural world, morality, and law. But later, disasters struck the land in the form of earthquakes, floods, volcanoes, and droughts. To protect themselves, the ancestors transformed into animals, plants, and rocks. The paths of these ancestors, who in their animal form roamed the land, have been passed from generation to generation.

Through the activities in this section, students will be exposed to a different understanding of the earth and how it was created. They'll also learn a storytelling technique developed in the arid Northern Territory of Australia, and imagine what they would have been in the Dreamtime.

The storybooks used in this unit are:

Meeks, Arone Ray. *Enora and the Black Crane*. New York: Scholastic, 1991.
Trezise, Percy. *Children of the Great Lake*. New York: HarperCollins, 1992.

❖ ACTIVITIES ❖

 ### STORY SUMMARIES

In *Enora and the Black Crane,* Enora is a young Australian living in the Dreamtime. One day Enora sees something in the bushes, and follows it into the forest. There he sees a circle of birds of all types, and shining colors that appear and flow over the birds, giving them bright colors. Enora hurries home, but no one in his family believes his story. So he decides to return to the clearing the next morning to bring back proof. He sneaks up on a crane that has just received its colors. Enora hits the bird with a stick, killing it, and brings it back to his family. But soon Enora begins to sprout black feathers. By the next morning he has transformed into a black crane, and must return to the forest to take his place among the other birds.

In *Children of the Lake,* three children belonging to the bird-dreaming live on the shores of the great lake. One day they make a raft to float out on the river to collect roots, fish, and crayfish. But a big wind comes up and pushes the raft out into the river. Days later, the children reach a small island where they make a hut and find food. But they are not alone: a deadly monster-snake lurks in the forest. They find a log that they make into a canoe, and set sail just as the monster-snake comes upon them. The children make their way back to their village, and everyone comes out to greet them.

 ### DISCOVERY/EXPLORATION

Among certain aboriginal groups in Australia, stories are told through drawings in the sand, sometimes using a boomerang to make the markings. Before the storyteller begins, the children gather around and shout "Djugurba!" ("Dreamtime!"). Have your students use a sandbox to tell/draw stories from their imaginations or to retell stories that you recite. Encourage them to create symbols, such as a house shape, to relate their tales. Finally, encourage the children to think about why the aborigines use sand in their storytelling by holding a discussion about the desert areas in Australia.

 ### LANGUAGE LINKS

The Australian aboriginal people believe that the Dreamtime ended when a series of natural disasters (floods, volcanoes, droughts, earthquakes) struck the land, and their ancestors had to transform into animals, plants, and even rocks to save themselves. Ask your students, "If there were a disaster, what would you most like to be?" The children might want to be a bird that could fly away, or a rock, because it could withstand the drought. Have the children write an explanation for the form they choose.

ANIMAL TALES

In 1770, British captain James Cook sailed into what is now Sydney harbor. Cook carried with him two famous botanists who went ashore and brought back specimens of plant and animal life. Cook was so impressed with their findings that he named the area Botanists' Bay. His voyage to Australia sparked an interest in Australian animals that continues today.

Many of the animal species brought back by Cook's botanists exist nowhere else in the world. Scientists believe that those animals, left in isolation for hundreds of thousands of years, evolved differently. The absence of placental animals, which pose a threat to marsupials (animals with pockets), has enabled the country to be populated with a wide variety of truly unique animals, including 125 species of marsupials. These animals range from the ostrich-sized, flightless emu to the world-famous koala bear to the animal that defies categorization, the duckbill platypus.

The Australian settlers' encounters with these animals in their new and unfamiliar environment is reflected in many storybooks. Among them are the storybooks used in this unit:

Base, Graeme. *My Grandma Lived in Gooligulch*. New York: Abrams, 1990.
Fox, Mem. *Possum Magic*. San Diego: Harcourt, 1983.

❖ ACTIVITIES ❖

STORY SUMMARIES

My Grandma Lived in Gooligulch is a rhyming tall tale about a grandmother who lives in a town in the outback with a population of 32. The town is famous because the grandmother's ranch is full of sometimes rowdy Australian animals. It's said that the woman has even taken a vacation by flying away in the beak of a pelican! While on that trip she went for a swim and disappeared, but some say she's back at Gooligulch.

In *Possum Magic*, two opossums, Grandma Poss and her grandson Hush, enjoy Grandma's magical powers, which can make Hush invisible. Then he can play with the other Australian animals unseen. But when Grandma wants to undo the spell, she must embark on a journey to find the right food to use.

DISCOVERY/EXPLORATION

Bring your students to Australia for a day! All that's needed are a few changes in your classroom:

• Before your students arrive, post your world map upside down. Known as the "corrected" map of the world, this is the way Australians see it!

• Welcome your students in the morning by saying, "G'day!"

• Give an Australian explanation of the seasons of the year, beginning with the sweltering months of December and January and moving on to the freezing temperatures of July and August. Discuss the different temperature of the southern hemisphere caused by the tilt of the earth on its axis. As the earth moves around the sun in its yearly rotation, the two hemispheres are closer to the sun at different times.

• Try out some Aussie slang! List words such as "barbie" (barbecue), "goffa" (soft drink), "uni" (university), "no worries" (no problem), "postie" (postman), "stickybeak" (busybody), "roo" (kangaroo), "mozzie" (mosquito), "mate" (best buddy), "chook" (chicken), and "bushranger" (crook, outlaw). Have students guess at their meanings. If they guess correctly, you can say, "Too right!" (exactly!).

LANGUAGE LINKS

Are you as "bald as a bandicoot" or as "cowardly as a dingo?" Many Australian animals have made their way into Australian slang. Students can practice using simile and learn about these animals by making up their own sayings. Discuss the physical and behavioral attributes of as many Australian animals as possible. Then have the students design their own similes. You may want to start them off with "hungry as a _____," "blind as a _____," "greedy as a _____," or "busy as a _____."

❖ PART 4 ❖

Europe

Named for Princess Europa, of Greek mythology, Europe, though not a large area, has had a pronounced influence on world culture. European inventions contributed to the industrial revolution of the 18th century, and European countries became the first to industrialize. Advances made throughout Europe have had a profound effect on human sciences, the arts, and literature.

Several of the traditions chosen for study in this chapter come straight from the European countryside. While modern Europe may be familiar, traditions rooted in rural lifestyles may be less so. Folklore, however, is a valuable tool with which to teach, and by reading stories quite literally "from the hearth," students can increase their understanding of European culture.

The topics covered in this chapter are:

• Ancient Greece. The Greeks believed in human-like gods, and enjoyed the dramatized versions of their exploits.

• Ireland. Your students may have heard of leprechauns, but do they know how to trap one? Or how to say hello in an all-but-lost language? The stories from Ireland will delight the entire class.

• Russia. The Baba Yaga tales, which have been told to Russian children for over 200 years, should fascinate their counterparts.

GREEK MYTHS

The myths of ancient Greece are an enduring part of our lives; many of the characters in them, such as Narcissus, have found their way into our vocabulary. In this unit, students will take a glimpse at these legends and the ancient society from which they came.

The gods of the Greek myths had many human attributes. They had weaknesses, such as jealousy and the need for revenge, but they were generally kind. Some were associated with forces of nature, some with human emotions, and others represented practical or leisure activities.

Greek myths were often transmitted through theater, which developed from a yearly festival of singing and dancing in marketplaces to plays with dialogue. In this later form, a chorus assumed the role of commentator; the chorus would warn the audience of events to come and sometimes give voice to the observations of the gods. If the play was a comedy, the chorus wore costumes, sometimes even dressing as animals.

The storybooks used in this unit are:

Martin, Claire. *The Race of the Golden Apples.* New York: Dial, 1991.
Yolen, Jane. *Wings.* San Diego: Harcourt, 1991.

❖ ACTIVITIES ❖

STORY SUMMARIES

In *The Race of the Golden Apples,* the goddess Diana finds a girl in the forest. The girl, Atalanta, has lived among the forest animals, but is ordered to return to her father's castle. When her father wants Atalanta to marry, the two agree that any man who can outrun her may become her husband; those who try but cannot will die. Hippomenes, who has loved Atalanta for years, begins the race. Just before she is to cross the finish line ahead of him, Atalanta pictures Hippomenes being led to his death, and lets him win.

Wings tells the legend of Daedalus, an Athenian inventor and artist whose downfall was his hubris (pride). Banished from Athens and imprisoned in Crete, Daedalus hatches a plan to escape—by air. He constructs wings from feathers and candle wax for his son Icarus and himself. But though he warns Icarus not to fly too close to the sun, Icarus does. The wax in his wings melts, and he falls to his death.

DISCOVERY/EXPLORATION

The ancient Greek mathematician Pythagorus discovered a property of music that we use to this day. Organize your students into pairs, and give each pair a rubber band. Have one student pull it taut (without overstretching it) and record the length on a piece of paper. Then have the other student pluck the band, and remember the sound it makes. Finally, have the students pull the rubber band to a length double that of the original, and pluck it again. How do the two sounds compare? Pythagorus noted that pulling a cord to double its original length made a sound one octave higher.

LANGUAGE LINKS

Drama was important in ancient Greece: it helped recount the legends of the past, as well as taught the audience how to behave in current society. The chorus, by speaking for the gods and forecasting the future, served critical functions.

Have your students create their own Greek chorus. Using familiar tales such as "Little Red Riding Hood" or "Cinderella," have them consider what a Greek chorus might say to the audience at different intervals. What, for example, would a chorus say when Cinderella's stepsisters treat her badly? And what would a chorus say while Little Red Riding Hood speaks to the wolf in his Grandma disguise? Divide students into groups of five or more and have them develop skits, based on their stories, using a Greek chorus. Have each group perform for the class.

IRELAND'S MIDDLE KINGDOM

Why do some people say "Bless you" when you sneeze? Though most people don't know it, they're scaring the fairies away. This Irish tradition comes from the belief that fairies play little tricks on people, like making us sneeze or trip. By saying "Bless you" we break their spell!

The Irish have many literary traditions, but a favorite around the world are the tales of the creatures of the land of the fairies, called the land of the Shee or the Middle Kingdom in Ireland. Here dwell leprechauns and other fairies, pookas and banshees.

Stories about the fairies are truly a living tradition—leprechaun and fairy sightings are still common in the Irish countryside. You're unlikely to see one, though, because leprechauns in particular are a bit resentful of teachers, who tend to believe the creatures don't exist. Leprechauns are rarely seen around schools!

The storybooks used in this unit are:

DePaola, Tomie. *Jamie O'Rourke and the Big Potato*. New York: Putnam, 1992.
McDermott, Gerald. *Daniel O' Rourke*. New York: Viking Penguin, 1986.

❖ ACTIVITIES ❖

STORY SUMMARIES

In *Jamie O'Rourke and the Big Potato*, Jamie is the laziest man in all of Ireland. When his wife falls ill, he's forced to find some means of support. He traps a leprechaun, whom he plans to extort for gold. But the leprechaun strikes a deal with Jamie: he gives him a wish, and Jamie wishes for a giant potato. He gets his wish, but the potato becomes a public nuisance when it rolls down the hill and blocks the road. The villagers remove the potato by eating it, and then all become sick of potato.

When *Daniel O'Rourke* goes to a party at a mansion on a hill, he has no idea of the adventures the night will bring. On his way home he passes a pooka and falls into a river. Then he washes up on an island, where he's rescued by an eagle, only to be abandoned on the moon. While falling back to earth he is caught by a flock of geese, who drop him into the ocean. Daniel is starting to be thrown high above the water by a whale spout when he's suddenly awoken by his wife. Had he fallen asleep next to the pooka?

DISCOVERY/EXPLORATION

"Erin Go Braugh," which means "Ireland forever," is an example of Irish Gaelic. Though nearly all Irish people now speak English, Gaelic was the original language of the land. It was spoken until the 19th century, when new policies forced the Irish people to speak English. Now the language is spoken only in isolated communities in the western regions of the country, but efforts are currently being made to revive Irish Gaelic through school instruction.

A bit of Gaelic lives on today in such words as smithereen, branch, tantrum, galore, shenanigan, bother, shamrock, and, of course, leprechaun. Post these words on a bulletin board and discuss their meanings with your class. Also have them consider the relationship between language and culture. What is a language? If we couldn't speak our native language, would it change the way we express ourselves?

LANGUAGE LINKS

Leprechauns are mischievous and often bring bad luck, but they make shoes for the fairies and are the richest of all Middle Kingdom creatures. If you want to catch a leprechaun you must keep your eye on him and demand gold. He'll never refuse if you keep watching him, but he'll try to trick you out of doing so. And if you look away for an instant, he'll be gone! Have your students write a set of instructions on how to catch a leprechaun.

RUSSIA'S BABA YAGA

On bitterly cold nights, Russian families are warmed by an enormous clay kitchen stove that reaches almost to the ceiling. According to tradition, this is the throne of the storyteller, who might sit on his perch and spin a tale of the famous old woman named Baba Yaga.

Baba Yaga is the much-loved star of hundreds of Russian folk tales. She is said to live in the darkest woods of Russia, in a small house that has chicken legs and turns at her command. She is also said to fly over the country in a mortar and pestle, sometimes accompanied by a big black cat, dog, or goose. She even has a broom, called a besom, which she uses to erase her tracks in the sky. Baba Yaga is sometimes a fearsome witch, and sometimes a kindly but misunderstood old woman.

The storybooks used in this unit are:

Arnold, Katya. *Baba Yaga*. New York: North South Books, 1993.
Ayres, Becky Hickox. *Matreshka*. New York: Bantam, 1992.

❖ ACTIVITIES ❖

 ## STORY SUMMARIES

In *Baba Yaga,* the old woman has a plan. In order to trick the young boy Tishka, she gets a special metal tongue that makes her sound like Tishka's mother. When Baba Yaga calls Tishka over to her house, he is trapped, and nearly becomes her dinner. But Tishka tricks Baba Yaga, escapes from the house, and hides in a tree. Baba Yaga gnaws at the trunk until the tree is about to fall. Tishka is saved by a goose flying by, which the boy takes home and keeps.

In *Matreshka,* Kata is a little girl who helps an old woman. In return, Kata is given a Matreshka doll, which she keeps in her pocket. On her way home, Kata encounters a great storm and seeks shelter—in the home of Baba Yaga. Kata soon finds that she is trapped there, and that Baba Yaga plans to turn her into a goose to add to a stew. But the Matreshka doll has magic powers and helps Kata escape by becoming smaller and smaller.

DISCOVERY/EXPLORATION

One of the most popular dishes in Russia is a soup called borsht. Like many foods eaten today, the recipe for it has been handed down through generations. Borsht is a soup based on beets and is quite simple to prepare. This recipe will serve four to six people.

> 3 bouillon cubes
> 4 cups boiling water
> 1 can shoestring beets
> 1 green onion, finely chopped
> 1 small cucumber, diced
> 1 hard-boiled egg, chopped
> 1/2 pint sour cream

Dissolve the bouillon cubes in the boiling water. Add the can of beets. Cool for 15 minutes. Add the green onion, cucumber, and egg. Blend in the sour cream. Chill for several hours. Borsht is served cold, but is often eaten with hot boiled potatoes.

LANGUAGE LINKS

Alexander Pushkin (1799-1837) is often called the Shakespeare of Russia. Famous for both his plays, novels, and children's stories, he is considered the first great author of modern Russia. Pushkin is perhaps best known for his novel in verse, *Eugene Onegin.* Your students can write in the style of this great author by retelling in verse form the storybooks used in this unit. Reread the stories, and summarize the plots together. Then have students write rhyming versions of the stories.

❖ PART 5 ❖

North America

Iroquois storytellers used a special method to remember tales. They carried sacks called Hage'ota: bags containing objects that represented the stories they could tell. Children would pull an object from the sack, and the storyteller would begin to tell his tale.

If we collected a sampling of North American stories, what might we find in the storyteller's bag? Perhaps a feather from an old headdress. Maybe a few yellowing immigration papers. There might even be a well-worn cowboy boot or a bit of woven cloth with an image of a bird.

We can take a hint about story presentation from Native Americans as well. As with many cultures' lore, Native American stories are transmitted orally. They belong not to the teller but to nature, and they have a life of their own. Stories should be told with dignity and spirit. And audiences should make the stories their own with comments and questions.

To help you teach this unit, consider the following information:

• When you look to the sky, what do you see? Native Americans see part of the history of the earth and the heavens.

• As students are exposed to the creation story of the Aztecs, help them see how the lessons in the story apply to us all.

• Sometimes it can help to stretch the truth a bit—especially if you're telling a tall tale! This unit paints a picture of the wild west.

• For centuries, families from every land have been pushed and pulled to the United States. The storybooks in this unit tell of this migration.

31

AZTEC LEGENDS

The Aztec empire lasted from the twelfth to the sixteenth century. From their capital, Tenochtitlan, in the Valley of Mexico, the Aztecs produced aqueducts, drawbridges, and hospitals that rivaled those of Europe at the time. The Aztecs were a society rich in tradition and myths.

One such myth heralded the end of their empire. The Aztecs believed that their god of wind, wisdom, and goodness, a tall, light-skinned man named Quetzalcoatl, had been chased away from the empire but would return in the year 1519. Miraculously, a tall, light-skinned man *did* arrive in 1519. But this man was Hernan Cortes, the Spanish explorer. Within two decades of his arrival, the Aztec empire was conquered by the Spanish.

In addition to their myths and legends, the Aztecs have left us many commonly used words, such as tomato, avocado, chocolate, and coyote. The activities in this unit will bring to life the stories of this ancient civilization.

The storybooks used in this unit are:

Lattimore, Deborah Nourse. *The Flame of Peace.* New York: McGraw Hill, 1987.
Rohmer, Harriet. *The Legend of Food Mountain.*
San Francisco: Children's Book Press, 1982. (bilingual)
Rohmer, Harriet, and Mary Anchondo. *How We Came to the Fifth World.*
San Francisco: Children's Book Press, 1988. (bilingual)

❖ ACTIVITIES ❖

STORY SUMMARIES

The Flame of Peace tells the story of the Aztec boy Two Flint, whose father goes off to negotiate with an army in the hills. When Two Flint's father is killed and his village prepares for war, Two Flint decides to try to find Lord Morning Star, the god of peace, who can stop the fighting. Two Flint sets out on his journey, and by using his wits brings the flame of peace from Lord Morning Star back to his village.

The Legend of Food Mountain tells about a part of the Aztec creation story in which the great god Quetzalcoatl creates the people of the earth. But the people were hungry and there was nothing to eat. Quetzalcoatl decided to give the corn from Food Mountain to the people, so he called upon the lightning god to use all of his strength to break open the mountain. But rain dwarfs appeared and stole the food. Since then the people have been calling on the rain gods to come back and return their food.

How We Came to the Fifth World describes another part of the Aztec creation story, telling of the four worlds the Aztecs believe existed before ours. In each world, food was plentiful, but men and women became greedy and the gods punished them by destroying the world.

DISCOVERY/EXPLORATION

Murals have been a colorful part of Mexican culture since the Aztec empire. Some depict historic events while others document daily life. After reading one or more of the creation myths in the stories above, have students design a mural for your classroom. First, discuss the stories and the kinds of images that might be seen in a mural depicting those times. What kind of food did the people eat? What kind of houses did they live in? What did they wear?

Use newsprint or tape together large pieces of paper to form a long strip for the mural. If students use paints, have them work on the floor to keep the paint from dripping. If the children use crayons, put the paper up first. Model the project by showing the students the murals of Diego Rivera, a famous contemporary Mexican muralist.

LANGUAGE LINKS

Myths have many functions: one is to teach young people how to become responsible members of a society. Have your students write an explanation of the lesson of each of the myths presented in the storybooks. What do these myths teach? What lessons are they passing on about how to live with others and with the earth?

COMING TO AMERICA

For hundreds of years, North America has been known as a place of refuge and opportunity. Each year it continues to draw immigrants and refugees from every corner of the world. It is this offer of hope and this mix of people that gives North America its distinct history and rich culture.

Immigrants come to North America for different reasons. Some are pushed by unfavorable conditions in their home countries; some are pulled by the promise of a better future or were forced to come as slaves. Most come for a combination of reasons.

In this chapter, students can learn about the decisions and circumstances that lead to a number of people's migration, as well as bring forth the wealth of stories that are waiting to be told in any North American classroom.

The storybooks used in this unit are:

Bresnick-Perry, Roslyn. *Leaving for America.*
San Francisco: Children's Book Press, 1992.
Bunting, Eve. *How Many Days to America?* New York: Clarion, 1988.
Surat, Michele Maria. *Angel Child, Dragon Child.* Milwaukee: Raintree, 1983.

❖ ACTIVITIES ❖

STORY SUMMARIES

Leaving for America is the autobiographical story of a Russian Jewish American girl named Roslyn as she and her mother prepare to reunite with Roslyn's father in the U.S. in 1922. The two say goodbye to friends and relatives, pack their belongings, and practice their English while Roslyn recalls adventures she shared with her cousin Zisl. On the day of Roslyn's departure, her grandfather asks her to promise to remain "a Jewish daughter" while in the United States. This is a promise she never forgets.

How Many Days to America? traces the journey of a strong Caribbean family. After hastily leaving their home because of political problems, the family spends days floating in a tiny boat, trying to reach the United States. The family run low on water and food, are robbed by pirates, and turned away when they first touch shore. But finally they reach the United States, where they eat their first Thanksgiving dinner.

In *Angel Child, Dragon Child,* Ut, a young Vietnamese American girl, struggles to get along in her new school while missing her mother, who remained in Vietnam. The other children make fun of her clothes and language, but Ut recalls her mother's caution to be an Angel Child. When Ut and a boy named Raymond get into a fight, the school principal orders Raymond to record Ut's story of her journey to America.

DISCOVERY/EXPLORATION

People come to America for many reasons. War, unemployment, slavery, or political persecution may push people out of their country. Conditions in America, such as economic opportunity or political freedom, may pull people there. Often it is a combination of these things that results in the journey. To dramatize this concept, brainstorm with the students a list of factors that might have pushed or pulled a family to America. Use the storybooks as examples, and make a list of "push factors" and a list of "pull factors" found in them. Discuss the terms "immigrant," "slave," "refugee," and "native."

LANGUAGE LINKS

Encourage all students to talk about the way their own family came to America by asking them to interview family members. Have them pose the questions, "What pushed our family to come to America? What pulled our family to America?" In class, ask each student to read his or her family's reasons aloud, and use this information as a starting point for discussion.

NATIVE AMERICAN STAR LEGENDS

It is said that Native American tribes had a story for each visible star. Some peoples used these legends as guides for behavior; some organized their villages like the patterns they saw in the sky; and others used the stars' positions to know when to plant. While the stories vary, all include a moral message for the audience.

The legends were originally passed down orally through a storyteller. On special occasions, the audience would sit in a circle around a fire, listening to the "carrier" of the story with rapt attention. Though respectful, the audience also participated with comments and questions, adding color and humor to the story. The storybooks in this unit can be read in the same spirit by assembling students in a circle and encouraging comments, questions, and even sound effects while you read.

The storybooks used in this unit are:

Esbensen, Barbara Juster. *The Star Maiden*. Boston: Little, Brown, 1988.
Mobley, Jane. *The Star Husband*. Garden City, NY: Doubleday, 1979.

❖ ACTIVITIES ❖

STORY SUMMARIES

In *The Star Maiden,* a brilliant star appears to the Ojibway (Chippewa) people. One young man learns through a dream that this star wishes to live among the people of the earth. The star is welcomed to earth in a dance by the village chief and wise ones, and soon rests in the form of a flower. But she is unhappy in this form, and finally settles on the river in the form of a water lily. Thus, the water lilies we see today are actually fallen stars from long ago.

In *The Star Husband,* a young Plains Indian girl wishes to gain immortality by having a star for a husband. She is granted her wish and ascends to the sky world, where she gives birth to a son, the moon. But she misses her village and decides to go home, leaving her husband and son in the sky. When she dies her spirit returns to the sky world, where she can still be seen.

DISCOVERY/EXPLORATION

Native American star legends can be used to teach about astronomy. Create a star chart of Native American constellations, showing the difference between those designated by the Greeks and those by Native American groups. Use the following list to guide your chart.

Greek Const.	Native American Const.	Group
North Star	Sky Coyote	Chumash, West,. U.S.
Big Dipper	7 boys transformed into geese	Chumash, West, U.S.
Orion's Belt	Crane and her sons	Tachiyokuts, West, U.S.
Corvus	Man with feet spread apart	Navajo, Southwest, U.S.
Tail of Scorpius	Rabbit tracks	Navajo, Southwest, U.S.
Corona Borealis	Circle of Chiefs	Pawnee, Great Plains, U.S.
Big Dipper	Bear and hunters	Micmac, N. Scotia, Can.
Milky Way	Cornbread dropped from mouth of running dog	Cherokee, Southeast, U.S.

LANGUAGE LINKS

Create a new universe in the classroom! Give each student a piece of black paper and have each make random or patterned dots of glue on it. Have the children sprinkle glitter over their paper and wipe off the excess (glow-in-the-dark paint may also be used). Then ask the students what they see in their constellation. Have them write a story about the figure they see. Be sure they include a moral. Post the finished stories. Invite each student to point out his or her constellation and tell the legend.

TALL TALES FROM THE WILD WEST

The tall tale is a style of story common to the United States, Canada, and Mexico that reached its peak in the early 1880's. It originated in the frontier days of North America: an era of exploration and expansion. The men, women, and children who made journeys into unknown territory during that time marveled at the terrain and the obstacles they encountered. This sense of wonder inspired fantastic stories.

While many tall tales are rooted in fact, their distinction is their exaggerated quality. Davy Crockett and Kit Carson were real people, but the legends that developed around them are fiction. Other heroes and heroines in tall tales never existed, yet they occupy a mythic role in our cultural history.

In the following activities, students are encouraged to learn about the culture of the frontier days through the period's legends. Students will study the stomping ground of frontier giants through a mapping exercise, and use their imaginations to see how far they can stretch the truth!

The storybooks used in this unit are:

Cohen, Caroll Lee. *Sally Ann Thunder Ann Whirlwind Crockett.*
New York: Greenwillow, 1985.
Small, Terry. *The Legend of Pecos Bill.* New York: Bantam, 1992.

❖ ACTIVITIES ❖

STORY SUMMARIES

The main character in *Sally Ann Thunder Ann Whirlwind Crockett* is a tough and fearless woman who "wore a beehive for a bonnet and a bearskin for a dress." When her husband, Davy Crockett, tires of bad man Mike Fink's bragging, Davy challenges Mike to scare his "sweet little wife." Mike sneaks up on Sally Ann in a crocodile suit, but he's no match for this tall-tale heroine.

The Legend of Pecos Bill is a rhyming tall tale of a man as wild as an animal. Among his many amazing feats, Bill harnesses a tornado and tames the wildest stallion. But Bill's lonely cowboy life seems finished when he meets Surefooted Sue, his match in bravery. Sue's toughness gets the better of her, though, and on their wedding day she rides Bill's stallion, only to be bucked straight to the moon.

DISCOVERY/EXPLORATION

Tall tales were written during an era of westward expansion. Students can learn about the context of these tales and practice their geography skills by making a map of tall-tale heroes and heroines. Post a map of the United States. Have each student draw a picture of a tall-tale hero or heroine, then tape the picture to the map in the area in which he or she lived.

LANGUAGE LINKS

Tall tales get their outrageous nature from exaggeration. Students can learn the technique of exaggeration by completing this exercise. First, discuss exaggeration and brainstorm examples in everyday speech. Then, ask students to help you fill in the blanks in a story by naming (1) a large animal, (2) a large piece of fabric (such as a blanket or tablecloth), (3) a faraway place, (4) a high number, and (5) a lake or river. Insert their answers into the following paragraph:

"When my brother Bob was born he was as big as a _____ (large animal). He had to use a _____ (large piece of fabric) for a diaper, and by the time he was five he could see from here to _____ (faraway place) on a clear day. For breakfast Bob ate an omelette made from _____ (high number) eggs, and could drink _____ (lake or river) dry in one gulp."

❖ PART 6 ❖

South America & Central America

The terrain of this area is truly fascinating: there are mountains, dense jungles, fertile pampas (treeless plains), deserts, and hot low-lands. The cultural landscape of this continent is just as interesting: this region was stumbled upon in the 15th century, and most of it was ruled by Spain and Portugal until the early 19th century.

The native cultures of pre-Columbian South America have now blended with European tradition to create what we think of as South American culture. The people of the area are largely mestizos—of mixed European and Indian descent—and some of the languages are mixtures of Spanish or Portuguese and Indian.

The result is a rich, diverse continent of new cultures and traditions. The storybooks and activities in this chapter will help to relay the exciting history of this region:

• At its height, the ancient Mayan civilization was perhaps the most advanced of the Americas. The storybooks used in this unit pay tribute to this society.

• The Spanish conquest of Latin America represents an important juncture in the history of these civilizations. Told from the perspective of the Indians, the storybooks demonstrate the European influence on the land.

• What remains of the ancient Latin American civilizations in the modern era? This unit's books and activities help inform students about the struggle to preserve what is left of those cultures.

MAYAN LEGENDS

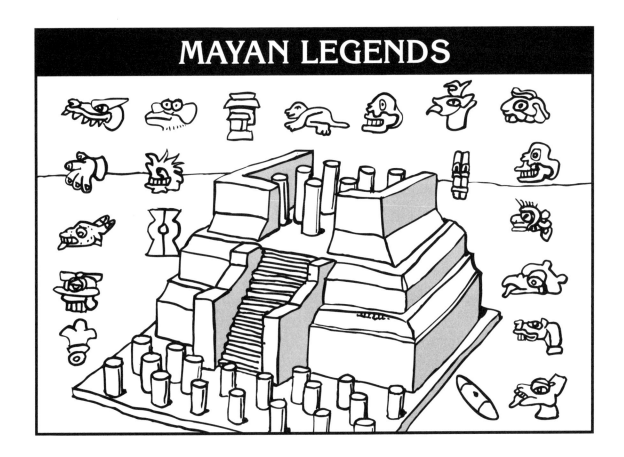

At its height, the Mayan civilization stretched over 125 square miles of what is now Mexico, Honduras, El Salvador, Guatemala, and Belize. The golden period, from 300 to 900 A.D., was a time of beautiful cities with enormous stone buildings carved out of dense jungle.

The Mayan people of that age had a well-developed calendar, a number system, and a written language based on hieroglyphs only recently decoded. They worshipped many gods, and believed that spirits existed in rocks, trees, rivers, and other elements of nature.

Foreign invasion drove the Mayan empire into decline, but Mayan leaders recorded information about their culture in writing. It is these records that have told us much of what we know about their society.

The storybooks used in this unit are:

Volkmer, Jane Anne. *Song of the Chirimia.*
Minneapolis: Carolrhoda Books, 1990. (bilingual)
Wisniewski, David. *Rain Player.* New York: Clarion, 1991.

❖ ACTIVITIES ❖

STORY SUMMARIES

In *Song of the Chirimia,* King Clear Sky has a daughter named Moonlight. Moonlight is charming and radiant, but she gradually grows unhappy. When she reaches the age of marriage, King Clear Sky calls for suitors. But no one can make Moonlight smile. Finally, a plain man arrives singing a song. Moonlight announces that if this man can sing like the birds she will accept his hand. The suitor departs for three moons and, with the help of the spirits, returns with a beautiful song. He wins Moonlight's hand in marriage.

In *Rain Player,* a priest consults his calendar and finds that the future holds a year of terrible drought. When he announces this news, a young man named Pik makes a snide remark that is overheard by the god Chac. Chac wagers the drought on a game of pok-a-tok, a soccer-like game. With the help of his teammates, Quetzal the Bird and Jaguar, Pik wins, and saves the land from drought for years to come.

DISCOVERY/EXPLORATION

The Mayans had a unique counting system. Unlike our system, which is based on the number 10, theirs was based on the number 20 and written horizontally, as shown below:

◯ = 0	•••• = 4	••• / — = 8	•• / — — = 12	• / — — — = 16	• ◯ = 20
• = 1	— = 5	•••• / — = 9	••• / — — = 13	•• / — — — = 17	
•• = 2	• / — = 6	— — = 10	•••• / — — = 14	••• / — — — = 18	
••• = 3	•• / — = 7	• / — — = 11	— — — = 15	•••• / — — — = 19	

Make math worksheets using this number system, and later have students make worksheets for each other.

LANGUAGE LINKS

The Mayans had a ritual called hetzmek, which is demonstrated in the storybook *Rain Player.* Hetzmek was a ceremony for three- and four-month-old children in which their godparents would present them with nine gifts for use later in life. For girls, two of these gifts were usually a weaving loom and a grinding stone. Among boys' gifts would be a planting stick and a coin. Often these gifts would have symbolic significance, representing courage or wisdom, for example. During the ceremony, the godmother would walk around the gifts with the child on her hip. Have students brainstorm a list of things they would give a baby if they were performing the rite of hetzmek. What values or ideas do the objects represent? Have students write out their list of objects and the values they represent.

THE SPANISH CONQUEST

When explorers such as Columbus and Cortes came to South and Central America in the 1500's, their arrival marked the beginning of an era of change for the peoples of the Americas. Guns, alcohol, and diseases began to tear at the fabric of those societies, as did the enslavement of the people and the misuse of natural resources.

The result is today's South and Central America, where the language is Spanish, the religion is a combination of Indian beliefs and Catholicism, and the people are a racial mixture of European and Indian.

Many pre-Columbian civilizations and their traditions are endangered or extinct. When Christopher Columbus landed on what is now Puerto Rico, in 1492, there were an estimated 300,000 Taino people. Fifty years later there were less than 500, and today there are no full-blooded Taino people alive. Such stories are tragic but crucial to an understanding of this region today.

The storybooks used in this unit are:

Rohmer, Harriet. *The Invisible Hunters.*
Novato, CA: Children's Book Press, 1987. (bilingual)
Rohmer, Harriet, and Jesus Guerrero Rea. *Atariba and Niguayona.*
Novato, CA: Children's Book Press, 1988. (bilingual)
Yolen, Jane. *Encounter.* New York: Harcourt, 1992.

❖ ACTIVITIES ❖

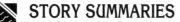

STORY SUMMARIES

In *The Invisible Hunters,* three brothers in Nicaragua discover a magical vine that makes them invisible. This power makes them great hunters, but the vine warns them never to sell their meat or use guns in their hunt. Soon, however, the brothers begin to use guns brought by foreigners, and the vine punishes them by making them invisible forever.

Atariba and Niguayona are young Taino friends. When the girl, Atariba, becomes sick, the boy, Niguayona, worries and searches for a cure. With the help of nature, Niguayona finds a cure, and the two children become important leaders among the Taino people.

Encounter tells the story of Columbus' arrival in Puerto Rico from the perspective of a Taino boy, one of the first Native Americans to greet the explorer. The boy has had a dream about the arrival of great white birds from the sea, and tries to warn his village about the dangers that lie ahead. No one listens, and his society begins to decline.

DISCOVERY/EXPLORATION

The Spanish conquest changed forever the cultures of Latin America *and* of Europe. For example, many foods that we use today were brought to Europe for the first time during this era. To illustrate the effects South American culture has had on the rest of the world, have your students go on a treasure hunt. Challenge each of them to search his or her house for items from South America. Send them searching for chocolate, corn, items made from rubber, avocados, tomatoes, potatoes, and yams. Make a classroom display of the treasures your students bring from home!

LANGUAGE LINKS

When the Spaniards encountered the Mayan civilization in the early 1500's, Mayan leaders feared cultural destruction and recorded their holy writings on wood bark and deerskin. One hundred and fifty years later, one such writing, the Popol Vuh, was discovered. This text has provided us with much of our understanding of Mayan civilization.

Have your students write their own Popol Vuh. Explain that creatures from another world have arrived in your land, and that you see great disaster for your civilization. To preserve some memory of your culture for future generations, you and your advisors have decided to write a record of your society. Have the students record information about their families, school, market, values, beliefs, legends, holidays, and traditions.

CULTURAL PRESERVATION

Latin America faces great challenges in preserving its traditions. Machine-made crafts threaten the trade of traditional craftspeople, and Indian languages, once spoken by all, are endangered as well. In some cases, entire societies are at risk. In particular, the destruction of the rain forests threatens the very livelihood of Indian peoples. When forests are cleared, the resources of communities disappear. Without a home, the people of the forest are likely to lose much of their culture.

Fortunately, there are movements to revive pre-Columbian culture. Associations are forming to teach and use native languages, and musical groups are experimenting with traditional instruments in order to recreate native music.

This unit offers students an opportunity to learn about efforts to preserve native culture and the environment, and to learn how they can help.

The storybooks used in this unit are:

Castaneda, Omar S. *Abuela's Weave*. New York: Lee and Low Books, 1993.
Dorros, Arthur. *Tonight Is Carnaval*. New York: Dutton, 1991.
Lewin, Ted. *Amazon Boy*. New York: Macmillan, 1993.

❖ ACTIVITIES ❖

STORY SUMMARIES

In *Abuela's Weave*, a young Guatemalan girl, Esperanza, tries hard to weave the way her abuela (grandmother) weaves. In their village, the two prepare items to take to the market in the city. Esperanza worries that their wares won't compete with the machine-made products they see, but buyers flock to purchase their traditionally made goods.

In *Tonight Is Carnaval,* the young Peruvian narrator of the story can't wait for the event. As he goes about his regular chores he dreams of playing the quena (lute) in the carnaval. Finally the evening comes and the festivities begin. Illustrations in this book show traditional embroidery.

Amazon Boy tells the story of Paulo, whose father cautions him that too much fishing in the river is causing a decline in the number of filhote fish. When Paulo catches a huge filhote he recalls his father's words, and throws the fish back.

DISCOVERY/EXPLORATION

The Inca Indians of Peru had no formal writing system, but recorded information using a device called a quipus. The quipus was an assembly of strings of different colors that the recorder would knot to register the history of a ruler's reign or figures from the Inca's population census.

Your students can learn about and help preserve this tradition of the quipus by making their own. Give each student a foot-long length of yarn of one color. Then give them shorter lengths of different colors. Students should tie the shorter lengths onto the longer one so that they hang as shown in the illustration on page 45. Have them choose a story they know well and have them designate certain strings for different characters. Students should make knots in the strings to represent events in the story; when two characters interact, their strings can be tied together. After they've finished knotting, the students can retell their stories to other members of the class.

LANGUAGE LINKS

Destruction of the rain forest threatens both the environment and the people who live there. Many items are now available that are or use rain forest products, such as Brazil nuts, cashews, gum made with chicle, chocolate, vanilla, bananas, and papayas. By using these products, we can ensure the maintenance of the forest. Bring in examples of these products.

❖ MORE MODELS ❖

AFRICA

Guthrie, Donna W. *Nobiah's Well*. Nashville, TN: Ideals, 1993.

Knutson, Barbara. *Sungura and Leopard: A Swahili Trickster Tale*. Boston: Little, Brown, 1993.

Steptoe, John. *Mufaro's Beautiful Daughters*. New York: Lothrop, Lee and Shepard, 1987.

ASIA

Gomi, Taro. *Coco Can't Wait*. New York: William Morrow, 1984.

Leaf, Margaret. *Eyes of the Dragon*. New York: Lothrop, Lee and Shepard, 1987.

Morimoto, Junko. *The Inch Boy*. New York: Puffin, 1986.

AUSTRALIA

Nunes, Susan. *Tiddalick the Frog*. New York: Atheneum, 1989.

Thiele, Colin. *Farmer Schulz's Ducks*. New York: Harper and Row, 1986.

Trezise, Percy, and Dick Roughsey. *Turramuli the Giant Quinkin*. Milwaukee: Gareth Stevens, 1988.

EUROPE

Fisher, Leonard Everett. *Theseus and the Minotaur*. New York: Holiday House, 1988.

Shute, Linda. *Tom and the Leprechaun*. New York: Lothrop, Lee and Shepard, 1988.

Silverman, Maida. *Anna and the Seven Swans*. New York: William Morrow, 1984.

NORTH AMERICA

Aardema, Verna. *Pedro and the Padre*. New York: Dial, 1991.

Dewey, Ariane. *The Tea Squall*. New York: Greenwillow, 1988.

Oughton, Jerrie. *How the Stars Fell into the Sky*. Boston: Houghton Mifflin, 1992.

Say, Allen. *Grandfather's Journey*. New York: Houghton Mifflin, 1993.

SOUTH AMERICA

Cherry, Lynn. *The Great Kapok Tree*. San Diego: Harcourt, 1990.

Dewey, Ariane. *The Thunder God's Son*. New York: Greenwillow, 1981.

Lattimore, Deborah Nourse. *Why There Is No Arguing in Heaven: A Mayan Myth*. New York: Harper and Row, 1989.

Markum, Patricia Maloney. *The Little Painter of Subana Grande*. New York: Bradbury Press, 1993.

❖ RESOURCES ❖

The following companies and organizations produce storybooks and instructional materials for teaching about world cultures. Contact them for catalogs of their products.

STORYBOOKS

Childrens' Book Press
1461 Ninth Avenue
San Francisco, CA 94122
tel.: (510) 655-3395
fax: (510) 655-1978

Colors of Harmony
5767 Foster Road
Bainbridge Island, WA 98110
tel.: (800) 283-5659

Troll Associates
Troll Multicultural Program
100 Corporate Drive
Mahwah, NJ 07498-0025
tel.: (800) 526-5289
fax: (201) 529-9347

INSTRUCTIONAL MATERIALS

American Friends Service
    Committee
15 Rutherford Place
New York, NY 10003

The American Forum for Global
    Education
45 John Street, Suite 1200
New York, NY 10038

Association for Supervision and
    Curriculum Development
1250 North Pitt Street
Alexandria, VA 22314

Catholic Relief Services
Global Education Office
209 West Fayette Street
Baltimore, MD 21201
tel.: (301) 625-2220

Center for Teaching International
    Relations
Publications Department
University of Denver
Denver, CO 80208

The National Geographic Society
Education Service, Department 90
Washington, DC 20036
tel.: (800) 368-2728

PC Globe, Inc.
4700 S. McClintock
Tempe, AZ 85282
tel.: (800) 255-2789

Social Science Education
    Consortium
855 Broadway
Boulder, CO 80302

Social Studies School Service
10200 Jefferson Boulevard, Room 6
P. O. Box 802
Culver City, CA 90232-0802

UNICEF
331 E. 38th Street
New York, NY 10016

World Affairs Materials
Box 726
Kennett Square, PA 19348